●●● Liz Driscoll

D1079178

Common
mistakes at

PET

.. and how to avoid them

CAMBRIDGE
UNIVERSITY PRESS

CAMBRIDGE UNIVERSITY PRESS
Cambridge, New York, Melbourne, Madrid, Cape Town, Singapore, São Paulo

Cambridge University Press
The Edinburgh Building, Cambridge CB2 8RU, UK

www.cambridge.org
Information on this title: www.cambridge.org/9780521606844

First published 2005
4th printing 2007

Printed in Dubai by Oriental Press

A catalogue record for this publication is available from the British Library

ISBN 978-0-521-60684-4 paperback

Contents

A, an or one?

1 Tick the correct sentence in each pair.

1. a I use a heater because my bedroom is really cold. ✓
   b I use an heater because my bedroom is really cold.
2. a We met one really nice boy when we were on holiday.
   b We met a really nice boy when we were on holiday. ✓

We use *an* before singular countable nouns beginning with a vowel *(a, e, i, o, u)*, and *a* before words beginning with the other letters of the alphabet:
*My friend is sharing **a room** with **an Italian girl**.*
☆ Note that we say *a university* (because it begins with a /j/ sound) and *an hour* (because the *h* is silent).

We also use *a* (or *an*) in expressions such as these:
*three times **a** week, **(a)** quarter of **an** hour*

We can use either *one* or *a* with *hundred, thousand* or *million*. We can also use *one* instead of *a* when we want to emphasise the number:
*There are **one hundred** centimetres in a metre.* (or ***a hundred** centimetres*)
*I've got two brothers and **one sister**.* (or *and **a sister***)

We use *one* and not *a* or *an* when we want to emphasise that we are talking about only one thing or person and not two or more:
*I invited three friends, but only **one of them** came.*
***One holiday** a year is not enough for me.*

2 Correct the mistake below.

I looked in my mirror and one white van was coming up behind me.

I looked in my mirror and .....a white van........ was coming up behind me.

3 Underline the correct word. In some sentences there are two possible answers.

1. I live on my own in <u>a</u> / an / one flat.
2. She's got a / an / <u>one</u> hundred euros.
3. We go there twice <u>a</u> / an / one month.
4. I went to the village with <u>a</u> / an / one friend.
5. She gave me a / an / <u>one</u> burger, not two.
6. I want to buy <u>a</u> / <u>an</u> / <u>one</u> umbrella. ✗
7. My cousin works at a / an / one university.
8. I've got <u>a</u> / an / <u>one</u> uncle and two aunts.

5

2 When do I use capital letters?

1 Tick the correct sentence in each pair.

1   a   I have an english exam next week.

✗   b   I have an English exam next week.

2 ✗ a   There is a trip to the exhibition in December.

     b   There is a trip to the exhibition in december.

We use capital letters with:

- titles and people's names: *Mrs Smith, Dr Lee , Queen Elizabeth II*
- members of the family when used as names: *Dad, Grandma*
- addresses: *Woodstock House, 16 West Road*
- letter beginnings and endings: *Dear Charlotte, Love from Emily, Yours sincerely*
- geographical names: *Rome (city), Spain (country), the Nile (river), the Pacific Ocean (ocean), Mount Everest (mountain)*
- nationality adjectives and languages: *English, Italian, French*
- days of the week: *Monday, Tuesday, Wednesday*
- months of the year: *January, February, March*
- festivals and special days: *Christmas Day, Valentine's Day, Easter*

☆ We use small letters in sentences when we are referring to someone's job or position rather than his / her name or title:
He is my doctor, The new queen is very young, This is my dad.

☆ We write only the pronoun *I* with a capital letter:
My sister and I went home, but then she went out again.

2 Correct the mistake below.

I've got a dentist's appointment on tuesday afternoon.

I've got ..~~a Dentist's~~ ..Tu... afternoon. ✗

3 Rewrite these sentences using small and capital letters.

1   madrid is in spain. *Madrid is in Spain.*

2   london is on the thames. *London is on the Thames*

3   are you learning italian? *Are you learning Italian*

4   my father is spanish. *My Father is Spanish*

5   i don't like mondays. *I don't like Mondays.*

6   my birthday is in may. *My Birthday is in May*

7   yours faithfully. paul may. *Yours Fai... May*

8   my mum is a doctor. *My Mum is a Doctor*

Do I need *am* / *is* / *are* in this sentence?

1 Tick the correct sentence in each pair.

1 a The person who sits next to me is called Natalia. ✓

   b The person who sits next to me called Natalia. ✗

2 a I may go to the cinema, but I am not sure. ✓

   b I may go to the cinema, but I not sure.

We use *am / is / are*:

- with an adjective to describe people and things:
  *My cousin **is tall**. He **is good-looking** too.*
- with *-ing* to form the present continuous:
  *I hope you **are feeling** well.*
- with *going to* to talk about the future:
  *I'm not **going to** go shopping on Saturday.*
- with the past participle to form the passive:
  *Cardiff and Swansea **are situated** in south Wales.*
- after *there* and *here*:
  ***There are** a lot of buildings near the school.*
  ***Here's** the book I promised you.*

☆ Note that we often use contractions (*'m*, *'s* and *'re*) in spoken and written English, especially after pronouns and short words.

2 Correct the mistake below.

Look at my shoes! I going to clean them.

Look at my shoes! I'm going to clean them.

3 Add *am, is* or *are* to these sentences.

1 I've got a new ruler because my old one broken. *my old one is broken*

2 I like this bag, but it too small for my things. *but it is too small*

3 Here our photos. Do you want to look at them? *Here is*

4 Paul works in New York and married to Anna. *and is married*

5 I like books which interesting. *which is in*

6 That all for now. I will write soon. *that is all*

7 I looking forward to seeing you. *I am looking*

8 Jack afraid his wife will fail her driving test. *is afraid*

1 Complete the phrases with *a* or *an*. Then rewrite the phrase with the adjective.

1 .... exam   .... *(hard)*
2 .... university   .... *(old)*
3 .... idea   .... *(interesting)*
4 .... house   .... *(unusual)*
5 .... restaurant   .... *(expensive)*
6 .... hour   .... *(extra)*
7 .... uncle   .... *(rich)*
8 .... lesson   .... *(easy)*

2 Rewrite the letter using capital letters where necessary. There are sixteen errors.

> 33 sandfield road
> oxford
> ox3 7rn
>
> february 10th 2005
>
> dear mrs brown
>
> please find enclosed a deposit for bed and breakfast accommodation for the weekend of march 15th. my husband and i look forward to seeing you then.
>
> yours sincerely
>
> barbara parker

3 Complete the text with *am, is* or *are*.

My name (1) .... Julie Wise and I
(2) .... 21 years old. I live in Spain, but I
(3) .... British. My parents (4) ....
English teachers in Madrid. I work in an office and
my sister (5) .... studying English at university.
Most of our friends (6) .... Spanish, but my
best friend (7) .... from Argentina. She (8)
.... a secretary in an international bank.

4 Write sentences using the notes. Use *is* or *are* and capital letters where necessary.

1 THE NILE / THE LONGEST RIVER IN AFRICA

....

2 CHINESE NEW YEAR / OFTEN IN JANUARY

....

3 NICOLE KIDMAN / AN AUSTRALIAN ACTRESS

....

4 JUVENTUS AND LAZIO / ITALIAN FOOTBALL TEAMS

....

5 KING LEAR / PLAY ABOUT AN OLD ENGLISH KING AND HIS THREE DAUGHTERS

....

6 THE HIMALAYAS / IN ASIA

....

7 SHOPS IN BRITAIN / OFTEN OPEN ON SUNDAY

....

8 LOS ANGELES / IN CALIFORNIA

....

5 Are the sentences right or wrong? Correct those which are wrong.

1 How deep is the pacific ocean? ....

2 I'm meeting one friend of mine later. ....

3 They not sure about the answer. ....

4 I've got some apples. Would you like one? ....

5 There is some people in the park. ....

6 I very tired today. ....

7 We're staying at the Ramsey Hotel. ....

8 See you in half a hour. ....

4 Singular or plural?

1 Tick the correct sentence in each pair.

1 a I'm going to have the most wonderful holiday of my life here.
  b I'm going to have the most wonderful holidays of my life here.
2 a I don't wear old cloths for work.
  b I don't wear old clothes for work.

Curtain or *curtains*?
We use *curtains* unless we are referring to one curtain only:
*I'd like to buy some new **curtains** for my room. (but The right **curtain** is longer than the left one.)*

Holiday or *holidays*?
We say *a holiday / on holiday* when we talk about a trip or a day off work. We can say *school holidays / summer holidays* to describe a period of time:
*I hope you enjoy your **holiday** in Britain.*

Mountain or *mountains*?
We use *mountains* when we talk about an area:
*My uncle's house is in the **mountains** near Turin.*

Cloth, cloths or *clothes*?
We use *clothes* to talk about things people wear. We say *an item* or *a piece of clothing* to describe one thing only. A *cloth* (plural *cloths*) is a piece of material for a particular purpose, e.g. *table cloth*, or for making clothes:
*I am going to buy some new **clothes** for the wedding.*

2 Correct the mistake below.

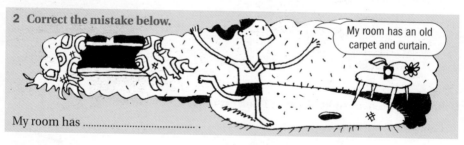

My room has an old carpet and curtain.

My room has ....

3 Complete the sentences with a singular or plural word from this page.

1 That ....*curtain*............ is torn, so I'm going to mend it.
2 During the summer .... , I worked in a shop.
3 I climbed the .... behind the house one morning.
4 Where's the .... for washing the dishes?
5 My bed cover is flowery, just like the .... at the windows.
6 Come and visit me for your next ....
7 I wore my new .... at the weekend.
8 I always take a map when I go to the ....

Plural or uncountable?

1 Tick the correct sentence in each pair.

1 a My feet are too small for these shoes.
  b My foots are too small for these shoes.
2 a I think Italian food is the best in the world.
  b I think Italian food are the best in the world.

Most plural nouns end in -s. However, some plural nouns are irregular:
My **neighbour** *is a wonderful* **person.** → *Our* **neighbours** *are wonderful* **people.**

Other irregular plural nouns include: *man* → *men, woman* → *women,*
child → *children, foot* → *feet, tooth* → *teeth, mouse* → *mice*
☆ *Police* and *staff* are also plural: *The* **police are** *hard-working.*

Some nouns have no plural form. We say that nouns such as *water* and *cheese* are
'uncountable' because we can't count them. We can only count *glasses / bottles of*
water and *pieces / slices of cheese.* Compare:
I'd like **some water**, *please.* and *I'd like* **a glass of water**, *please.* (not ~~two waters~~)

Other common uncountable nouns include *food, furniture, hair, homework,*
information, money and *work.* We use singular verbs with uncountable nouns:
The **furniture** *in my bedroom* **looks** *good.*
My **hair** *is dark brown.* (but *I've got* **one** *grey* **hair** *behind my ear.*)

2 Correct the mistake below.

Can you buy me a newspaper?
There are some money on the table.

Can you buy me a newspaper? .... on the table.

3 Underline the correct form.

1 Here *is / are* some information about hotels in Paris.
2 Some children *is / are* afraid of dogs.
3 There *was / were* a bottle of water in the fridge.
4 The staff *is / are* on a training course.
5 The *woman / women* is reading the newspaper.
6 Your *hair looks / hairs look* very nice.
7 How many *slices of bread / bread* have you got?
8 This homework *was / were* easy.

11

6 When do I use *of* and when do I use an apostrophe?

1 Tick the correct sentence in each pair.

1 a We spent two days in my grandmother's house.
   b We spent two days in the house of my grandmother.

2 a Look at the top of the page.
   b Look at the page's top.

We use apostrophe + *s* (*'s*) to talk about things associated with one person:
*My **friend's** name is Natalia.*
*These are my **husband's** things.*

We use *s* + apostrophe (*s'*) to talk about things associated with more than one person:
*Here is my **friends'** teacher.*
*The **students'** records are in the cupboard.*
☆ Note that we use an apostrophe + *s* (*'s*) with irregular plural nouns:
*The **children's** party is at the club.*

We also use apostrophe + *s* (*'s*) on its own:
*My birthday is the same day as my **mother's**.*

We use *of* to talk about things associated with places and objects:
*Rome is the capital **of Italy**.* (not ~~Italy's capital~~)
*The answers are at the back **of the book**.*

2 Correct the mistake below.

These are my parents. And this is the best friend of my mother.

These are my parents. And this is ....

3 Write possessive sentences using the words in brackets.

1 I visited .....my friend's school..... *(school / my friend).*
2 We stayed in .... *(other house / her family).*
3 'Garden Designs' is .... *(name / his company).*
4 It's .... *(birthday / my little brother).*
5 .... *(cousins / my father)* live in Argentina.
6 They are .... *(brothers / my best friend).*
7 .... *(phone numbers / my friends)* are in this book.
8 I found .... *(glasses / man).*

12

TEST 2

1 Insert an apostrophe where necessary.

1 The babys clothes are in the cupboard. ....
2 My English isn't as good as my wifes. ....
3 Do you know your neighbours very well? ....
4 My friends names are Roberto and Giorgio. ....
5 Have you got the address of the hotel? ....
6 My teachers family comes from Scotland. ....
7 Look at that boys shoes! ....
8 Have you got the childrens things? ....

2 Add the plural ending -s where necessary.

1 My parents didn't enjoy their holiday. ....
2 The staff were all very nice. ....
3 I like your new curtain. ....
4 Two police officer came to the door. ....
5 My front tooth hurts! ....
6 I like going to the Scottish mountain in winter. ....
7 When did you get your hair cut? ....
8 I'll wash those dirty dish cloth. ....

3 Rewrite these sentences in the plural form.

1 This is the man's book.
   These ....
2 The furniture in the bedroom is quite old.
   The ....
3 His book is on the desk.
   Their ....
4 Do you know that woman over there?
   Do .... ?
5 Is that your friend's jacket?
   Are .... ?
6 The boy is doing his homework.
   The ....
7 This new car is quite nice.
   These ....
8 Which child wears glasses?
   Which ....

4 Write two sentences for each picture. Use *some* in the first sentence and one of the words in the box in the second.

| bar | bottle | cup | glass | jar | loaf | packet | piece |

1 I'd like ....
....

2 Can I have .... ?
....

3 Would you like .... ?
....

4 Could I have .... ?
....

5 Do you want .... ?
....

6 Shall I get .... ?
....

7 Did you buy .... ?
....

8 I'm going to buy ....
....

5 Are the sentences right or wrong? Correct those which are wrong.

1 Which cloths are you wearing for the party? ....

2 Can I have some informations about this course? ....

3 My brother's girlfriend is from New Zealand. ....

4 There are some food in the fridge. ....

5 Where's your homework? ....

6 I eat a fruit every day. ....

7 Who sits at the class's front? ....

8 This is my grandparent's can. ....

7 What's the negative form of *have*?

1 Tick the correct sentence in each pair.

1 a I don't have dinner with my parents very often.
   b I haven't dinner with my parents very often.
2 a We didn't have got enough money to buy a drink.
   b We didn't have enough money to buy a drink.

We use either *have* or *have got* when we talk about our possessions, families, personal characteristics and ailments. Remember that we use *has* or *has got* with *he, she* and *it*:
*I **have** a lot of clothes. I've **got** a lot of clothes.*
*My mother **has** a cousin in Australia. My mother **has got** a cousin in Australia.*

The negative forms are *don't / doesn't have* and *haven't / hasn't got*:
*I **don't have** a camera.* (not *I **haven't** a camera.*)
*My room **hasn't got** much furniture.* (not *My room **hasn't** much furniture.*)

We use *have* (also *don't have / doesn't have*) for actions:
*I **don't have** breakfast in the morning.* (not *I **haven't** breakfast*)
*He **has** a shower every morning.* (not *He **has got** a shower*)

The past tense of *have* and *have got* is *had*. The negative is *didn't have*:
*I've **got** a terrible headache. I wasn't well yesterday, but I **didn't have** a headache.* (not *I **hadn't** a headache, I **hadn't got** a headache* or *I **didn't have got** a headache*)

The future form is *will ('ll) have*. The negative form is *won't have*:
*If you take this tablet, you **won't have** a headache.*

2 Correct the mistake below.

My room hadn't a TV when I moved in, so I bought one.

My room .... when I moved in, so I bought one.

3 Tick (✓) the sentences which are correct. In some pairs both sentences are correct.

1 a I don't have much money. ....✓....
   b I haven't got much money. ....✓....
2 a We didn't have got a good holiday. ....
   b We didn't have a good holiday. ....
3 a He didn't have fun at the party. ....
   b He hadn't got fun at the party. ....
4 a My parents don't have a car. ....
   b My parents haven't got a car. ....
5 a I didn't have a job last year. ....
   b I hadn't got a job last year. ....
6 a My sister doesn't have a boyfriend. ....
   b My sister hasn't got a boyfriend. ....
7 a I hadn't my glasses with me. ....
   b I didn't have my glasses with me. ....
8 a My brother doesn't have red hair. ....
   b My brother hasn't got red hair. ....

Present simple or present continuous?

1 Tick the correct sentence in each pair.

1 a I'm going to the club every evening.
  b I go to the club every evening.

2 a My father's got a good job. He's working for an international bank.
  b My father's got a good job. He works for an international bank.

We use the present simple to talk about:
- permanent states: *I **don't live** near an underground station.*
- regular habits: *I **play** football most weekends.*
- general truths: *Garage mechanics **repair** cars.*

We use the present continuous to talk about current actions or events that are unfinished:
- to describe what is happening at the time of speaking:
  *Can you switch the TV off? I**'m not watching** it.*
- to describe temporary actions, often with *today, this week*, etc. to show the period of time:
  *I**'m walking** to school this month. It's good for me.*
- to describe ongoing actions which are happening around this time but not necessarily at the time of speaking:
  *I**'m learning** English because I want to work in a travel agent's.*

2 Correct the mistake below.

I'm on a diet. I don't eat very much this week.

I'm on a diet. .... this week.

3 Complete the sentences with the present simple or present continuous form of *play, read, wear* and *work.*

1 My sister .... *works* .... as an air stewardess for Alitalia.
2 Children in Britain usually .... school uniform.
3 I .... a book about the history of Rome. It's very interesting.
4 Some of the best footballers in the world .... for Real Madrid.
5 I .... my new shoes today.
6 My father .... travel books in his free time.
7 Lucia's in her bedroom. She .... a game on the computer.
8 I .... really hard this month.

16

Which verbs don't have a continuous form?

1 Tick the correct sentence in each pair.

1 a I think this spaghetti is great. *I think this spaghetti is great*

  b I'm thinking this spaghetti is great.

2 a I don't know the answer to the question. *I don't know the answer to the question*

  b I'm not knowing the answer to the question.

We do not use the continuous form with the following verbs which describe thoughts and feelings: *believe, depend, forget, hate, know, like, love, mean, need, prefer, remember, understand, want*

Some common verbs have more than one meaning. We do not use the continuous form when *think* means *believe* and when *have* refers to possession. Compare:
*I **think** it's going to rain soon.* and *I'm **thinking** about becoming a teacher.*
*My sister **has** a new car.* and *She isn't at home now. She's **having** a driving lesson.*

We do not usually use the continuous form with *hear, smell* and *taste*. We can use *seeing* when it refers to meeting someone in the future. We often use *can* with *hear, smell, taste* and *see* to describe what is happening now. Compare:
*I **(can) see** two women in the picture.* and *I'm **seeing** my sister tomorrow evening.*

We use both the continuous and simple form of *look* and *feel* to talk about now:
*You're **looking** tired. What's the matter?* and *You **look** tired. What's the matter?*
*I'm **feeling** nervous about my exams.* and *I **feel** nervous about my exams.*

2 Correct the mistake below.

This room is smelling of fish.

This room .... fish.

3 Tick (✓) the sentences which are correct. In some pairs both sentences are correct.

1 a I'm liking to get up early. ....   b I like to get up early. ......✓......

2 a What is this word meaning? ....   b What does this word mean? ....

3 a How are you feeling? ....   b How do you feel? ....

4 a I'm not needing anything, thank you. ....   b I don't need anything, thank you. ....

5 a I'm thinking about buying a car. ....   b I think about buying a car. ....

6 a This soup is tasting really nice. ....   b This soup tastes really nice. ....

7 a My mother is looking tired. ....   b My mother looks tired. ....

8 a I'm not having blue eyes. ....   b I don't have blue eyes. ....

TEST 3

1 Rewrite these sentences in the negative form.

1 My new coat has got a belt. ....

2 I've got three cousins. ....

3 We had dinner at home yesterday evening. ....

4 I'll have a cup of coffee. ....

5 My mum has got a sore throat. ....

6 I have a shower every morning. ....

7 My brother has a girlfriend in America. ....

8 I had flu last winter. ....

2 Choose the correct form.

1 I *'m trying* / *try* not to eat chocolate this week.

2 Can you answer the phone? I *'m making* / *make* the dinner.

3 John *'s going* / *goes* to the cinema two or three times a month.

4 This spaghetti *is tasting* / *tastes* delicious!

5 I *'m reading* / *read* a book about Picasso at the moment.

6 Children in some countries *aren't going* / *don't go* to school.

7 Please be careful! I *'m having* / *have* a broken arm.

8 My English *is improving* / *improves*.

3 Complete the sentences with the correct form of the verb.

1 My dad .... *(try)* to learn the guitar, but he ....
   (not want) to have lessons.

2 Can you change the CD? I .... *(not enjoy)* this music. I
   .... *(want)* to listen to a different CD.

3 My sister .... *(need)* a new bike. She .... *(use)*
   mine at the moment.

4 My brothers .... *(play)* football twice a week, but they
   .... *(not like)* watching it on TV.

5 I .... *(think)* about buying a digital camera. I
   .... *(believe)* they're not too expensive.

6 Be quiet! I .... *(watch)* this film. I .... *(not
   make)* a noise during your favourite TV programmes.

7 That's a nice perfume you .... *(wear)* today.
   It .... *(smell)* very nice.

8 My mum isn't here at the moment. She .... *(have)* lunch with a
   friend, I .... *(think)*.

4 Complete the postcard. Use the present simple, present continuous or *can* + infinitive form of the verbs in the box.

go	have	hear	know
see	sit	stay	work

Dear Lauren

I (1) .... a great time in London. I (2) ....
with my aunt. She (3) .... in London for a year and invited me to
visit her. Her flat is on the tenth floor and I (4) .... the Tower
of London from my bedroom window. I (5) .... somewhere
interesting every day and I went to the Tower yesterday. It's one o'clock now and I
(6) .... in Green Park. I (7) .... the sound
of a fire engine. I (8) .... I switched the kettle off this morning,
so I don't think the fire's in my aunt's flat!

Love, Katy

Welcome to London

5 Are the sentences right or wrong? Correct those which are wrong.

1 You look great in that jacket! ....

2 We always have got a party at the end of term. ....

3 You can borrow this pen. I'm not needing it. ....

4 Birds are making their nests in spring. ....

5 I hadn't got a cold last winter. ....

6 Do you prefer dark or milk chocolate? ....

7 I wear my new jeans today. ....

8 We're thinking the shops will close soon. ....

Regular or irregular past simple forms?

1 Tick the correct sentence in each pair.

1 a They paid four euros for the tickets.
  b They payed four euros for the tickets.
2 a My feet fell cold when I put them on the floor.
  b My feet felt cold when I put them on the floor.

Regular past simple forms end in -*ed*:
*clean → clean**ed**, play → play**ed**, arrive → arriv**ed***
*try → tr**ied**, carry → carr**ied**, tidy → tid**ied***
*plan → plan**ned**, slip → slip**ped**, rob → rob**bed***

Some verbs have irregular past simple forms:
*go → **went**, find → **found**, pay → **paid**, say → **said**, buy → **bought**, bring → **brought***

Some verbs have the same past simple form and infinitive form:
*let → **let**, put → **put**, cost → **cost**, read* /riːd/ *→ **read** /red/*

Some irregular past simple forms are easily confused:
*My uncle **brought** his wife with him.* (bring)
*We **bought** many presents when we were on holiday.* (buy)
*I slipped and **fell** down the stairs.* (fall)
*I got out of bed because I **felt** better.* (feel)

2 Correct the mistake below.

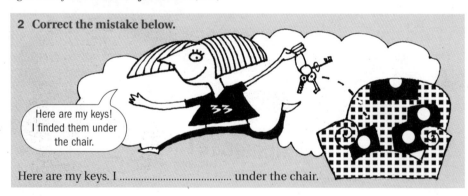

Here are my keys!
I finded them under the chair.

Here are my keys. I .... under the chair.

3 Complete the sentences with the past simple form of the verb.

1 I don't know how the lamp ....*fell*............... (*fall*) down.
2 Did you understand what she .... (*say*)?
3 I .... (*cut*) my leg when I slipped.
4 My aunt .... (*live*) in Toronto for many years.
5 This is a present my father .... (*bring*) me from Rome.
6 I .... (*stay*) in a hostel when I first arrived here.
7 My friends .... (*buy*) me a new watch.
8 My uncle .... (*study*) in New York and then worked there.

20

How do I form the past simple negative?

1 Tick the correct sentence in each pair.

  1 a John didn't drink his cup of tea.

      b John didn't drank his cup of tea.

  2 a I didn't went to the cinema at the weekend.

      b I didn't go to the cinema at the weekend.

We use *did not (didn't)* + the infinitive of the verb when we form the past simple negative. The main verb stays in the infinitive:

*I played tennis every day last week, but I **didn't play** yesterday.* (not *I ~~didn't played~~*)

*It rained a lot in April, but it **didn't rain** much in May.* (not *it ~~didn't rained~~*)

Irregular verbs also use the infinitive in the negative:

*She went to the dentist yesterday morning, so she **didn't go** to work.*

*I **didn't have** time to go shopping yesterday.* (not *I ~~hadn't time~~*)

☆ We say *didn't have* (not *~~hadn't~~*) (see Unit 7).

Some irregular verbs have the same infinitive and past simple form:

*I cut my nails every week. I **didn't cut** them at the weekend, so I **cut** them today.*

*My sister **put** my books on the chair. She **didn't put** them on the table.*

The verb *read* has the same infinitive and past simple form, but different pronunciation:

*I **read** /red/ a magazine on the train this morning. I **didn't read** /riːd/ a newspaper.*

2 Correct the mistake below.

> Paul's very tired because he didn't slept well last night.

Paul's very tired .... last night.

3 Rewrite these positive sentences in the negative form.

  1 We went to the cinema at the weekend. ....*didn't go*...........

  2 I played very well in our last match. ....

  3 Susie stayed out very late last night. ....

  4 Stefan told his family what had happened to him. ....

  5 I heard the news about your brother this morning. ....

  6 They got married in church. ....

  7 I expected you to wait for me. ....

  8 The man who found the ring returned it. ....

Past simple or past continuous?

1 Tick the correct sentence in each pair.

1 a When I was a child, I was going to the village school.
  b When I was a child, I went to the village school.
2 a I was playing football when I hurt my knee.
  b I played football when I hurt my knee.

We use the past simple to talk about completed actions or events in the past. We also use the past simple to describe a permanent state and regular habits:
*I **watched** the news on TV last night. At half past ten I **went** to bed.*
*My father **worked** in London for fifteen years. He **walked** to the office every day.*

We use the past continuous to refer to a particular moment and a temporary state:
*I **was watching** the news on TV at ten o'clock last night.*
*I was in America last summer. I **was working** at a sports camp.*

We use the past simple and past continuous together when something happened in the middle of something else. We use the past continuous for two things happening at the same time and the past simple when one thing happened after another. Compare:
*I **was watching** TV when the phone **rang**.*
*My brother **was getting** ready for bed while I **was watching** TV.*
*When the phone **rang**, my brother **answered** it. He **knew** it would be his girlfriend.*
☆ Some verbs are not normally used in the continuous (see Unit 9).

2 Correct the mistake below.

Hello, Sam. I went out when the phone rang.

Hello, Sam. I ....

3 Underline the correct form.

1 My brother *decided* / *was deciding* to decorate his flat.
2 I *broke* / *was breaking* my arm when I was twelve years old.
3 Last summer I *went* / *was going* to Ireland by plane. It was fun.
4 I *did* / *was doing* the shopping when I lost my purse.
5 When I passed my driving test, I *bought* / *was buying* a car.
6 I *sat* / *was sitting* on the underground at eight o'clock this morning.
7 We *didn't understand* / *weren't understanding* the instructions.
8 I *won* / *was winning* three prizes in the competition.

TEST 4

1 **Read the first text. It describes what Pete does every day. Complete the second text with the past simple.**

Every day …
'I get home from work at six o'clock every day. I watch the news on TV and then make my dinner. I put the dishes in the dishwasher, then I read the newspaper and do the crossword. When I feel tired, I go to bed.'

Yesterday …
'I (1) .... home from work at six o'clock yesterday. I (2) .... the news on TV and then (3) .... my dinner. I (4) .... the dishes in the dishwasher, then I (5) .... the newspaper and (6) .... the crossword. When I (7) .... tired, I (8) .... to bed.'

2 **Complete the sentences with a negative form from the box of the past simple.**

cost	feel	find	get	have	know	take	want

1 I left my camera at home, so I .... any photos.
2 Alex bought a mobile phone. It .... very much.
3 It was my birthday last week, but I .... a party.
4 Jane looked everywhere for her watch, but she .... it.
5 Suzy .... very well yesterday, so she stayed in bed all day.
6 We had a great holiday. We .... to come home.
7 My teacher asked me a question, but I .... the answer.
8 John went for an interview, but he .... the job.

3 Look at the pictures. They show what Ben and Katie did yesterday. Complete the sentences with positive and negative forms of the past simple.

Ben

Katie

1 Katie .... tennis.
2 Ben .... to the radio.
3 Katie .... her friends.
4 Ben .... at 7.30 am.
5 Katie .... the dishes.
6 Ben .... a letter.
7 Katie .... the shopping.
8 Ben .... jogging.

4 Complete the sentences using the past simple and past continuous.

1 I was waiting for the bus when my sister .... past. *(drive)*
2 When I opened the door, two children .... there. *(stand)*
3 I arrived at work at 9.30 am and my boss .... at his desk. *(sit)*
4 When the film finished, I .... the TV off. *(switch)*
5 This time last year I .... in New York. *(live)*
6 I had a shower, then .... on my new clothes. *(put)*
7 My cousin .... her glasses when I saw her. *(wear)*
8 While I was having a shower, the water .... cold. *(go)*

5 Are the sentences right or wrong? Correct those which are wrong.

1 My parents hadn't a car when they got married. ....
2 I was having a bad dream and falled out of bed. ....
3 Paul can't cook because his mother didn't teach him. ....
4 My parents were here, but they didn't stayed long. ....
5 We were starting French lessons two months ago. ....
6 I cut my hand while I was chopping onions. ....
7 My boss skied in Italy when he broke his leg. ....
8 I buyed this new jacket in the sales. ....

How do I use personal pronouns?

1 Tick the correct sentence in each pair.

1 a That scooter isn't my, so I don't use it.
   b That scooter isn't mine, so I don't use it.
2 a He showed my how the club works.
   b He showed me how the club works.

We use *my, your, his, her, its, our* and *their* with a noun:
My bedroom *is the smallest.*
She left **her handbag** *on the train.*

We can use *mine* instead of *my* + noun when we refer to the same thing again in a sentence. Remember that we use *yours, his, hers, ours, theirs* in the same way:
The smallest bedroom is **mine**. *The largest one is* **yours**.

We use *me, you, him, her, it, us, them*:
- as the object of a verb:
  I hope you'll **bring me** *a surprise.*
- after a preposition such as *for, to, with*:
  The teacher had some advice **for them**.

2 Correct the mistake below.

I'm pleased I brought this umbrella with my!

I'm pleased I brought this umbrella .... !

3 Complete the sentences with an appropriate personal pronoun.

1 The coach told .... *me* .... that I'm a good player.
2 My sister painted the furniture because it's ....
3 We bought two maps, but only one was for ....
4 My mum left a message on my mobile, so I phoned .... back.
5 The students asked their teacher and she let .... go.
6 My boyfriend phoned and I told .... about my exam.
7 My friend's got a new camera, but I prefer ....
8 Here are your certificates, but we can't find ....

How do I use reflexives?

1 Tick the correct sentence in each pair.

1 a My girlfriend and I live in different cities. We phone each other every day.
   b My girlfriend and I live in different cities. We phone us every day.
2 a When I got home, I made myself a cup of coffee.
   b When I got home, I made me a cup of coffee.

We use *me, you, him, her, it, us, them* as the object of a verb:
*My uncle came to visit **me** for three days.*
*Our teacher is great. We like **him** a lot.*

See Unit 13 for other examples.

We use *myself, yourself, himself, herself, itself, ourselves,* yourselves and *themselves*
when the subject and object of a verb are the same:
*I was angry with **myself** when I lost my watch.*
*Take care of **yourself**.*
***We** went out and bought **ourselves** a drink.*
***They** introduced **themselves** by saying where they came from.*

We use *each other* when two (or more) people do the same thing to the other. We often
use *each other* with *(get to) know, like, meet, phone, see, tell, understand, write*:
*I hope **we**'ll see **each other** soon, Sarah.*
*Everyone in the class knows **each other** very well.*

2 Correct the mistake below.

I work with that woman, but we don't like us.

Woof!

dog news

I work with that woman, but we ....

3 Underline the correct word.

1 Last lesson we all said something about *us / ourselves* and our families.
2 I share a flat with a student from Madrid. We know *us / each other* quite well.
3 When Susan lost her key, she hated *her / herself*.
4 I asked *me / myself* what I should do.
5 There are twelve of *us / ourselves* in the class.
6 My friends send *them / each other* text messages all the time.
7 You should get *you / yourselves* mountain bikes before we go on the trip.
8 My parents went to New York, but they didn't enjoy *each other / themselves*.

Many, much or a lot of?

1 **Tick the correct sentence in each pair.**

1 a   I hope many people will come to the disco.
   b   I hope a lot of people will come to the disco.
2 a   My teacher is organising a concert with much music.
   b   My teacher is organising a concert with a lot of music.

We use *many* with countable nouns and *much* with uncountable nouns in negative
statements and questions:
*I didn't have **much fun** at the party.*
*Did you take **many photos** when you were on holiday?*

We sometimes use *a lot of* in positive and negative statements and questions, in
informal and spoken English, though it is not considered correct in written and
formal English:
*I tried on **a lot of clothes** in the shop.*
*I didn't have **a lot of fun** at the party.*
*Did you take **a lot of photos** when you were on holiday?*

We use *a lot* without a noun:
*The teacher told me **a lot** about his experiences.*

We use *much* without a noun in negative statements and questions:
*The lesson was interesting, but we didn't learn **much**.*
*Do you use the Internet **much**?*

2 **Correct the mistake below.**

I have much work to
do before I go home.

I have .... home.

3 **Tick (✓) the sentences which are correct. In some pairs both sentences are correct.**

1 a   There are a lot of chairs in the
       room. ......✓......
2 a   I didn't buy a lot of pens. ....
3 a   Do you know a lot about plants? ....
4 a   I like places with a lot of people. ....
5 a   Sorry, I haven't got a lot of time. ....
6 a   I cooked a lot of Italian food. ....
7 a   I like tea, but I don't drink a lot. ....
8 a   Do you read a lot of books? ....

1 b   There are many chairs in the room.
       ....
2 b   I didn't buy many pens. ....
3 b   Do you know much about plants? ....
4 b   I like places with many people. ....
5 b   Sorry, I haven't got much time. ....
6 b   I cooked much Italian food. ....
7 b   I like tea, but I don't drink much. ....
8 b   Do you read many books? ....

1 **Rewrite the sentences in the negative form. Use *much* and *many*. Which sentence in each pair is true for you?**

1 I do a lot of homework. ....

2 I've got a lot of clothes. ....

3 I do a lot of sport. ....

4 I work with a lot of people. ....

5 I know a lot about football. ....

6 I go to the theatre a lot. ....

7 I watch a lot of videos. ....

8 I eat a lot of pasta. ....

2 **Put the words in the correct order to make sentences.**

1 him / can / show / classroom / to / his / I

....

2 for / want / lunch / I / don't / much

....

3 up / she / introduced / stood / herself / and

....

4 use / my / or / yours / pen / you / can

....

5 her / didn't / very / they / like / much

....

6 them / a / she / had / surprise / for

....

7 interesting / stories / the / are / our / most

....

8 lot / weekend / I / did / at / the / a

....

3 **Complete the sentences with possessive adjectives (*my, our*, etc.) and possessive pronouns (*mine, ours*, etc.).**

1 Can you lend me .... pen?

2 Where are your coats? We put .... in the bedroom.

3 Is your sister having a party for .... birthday?

4 I don't like my job, but my friends like ....

5 My brother and I live with .... parents.

6 Have you got a dictionary? I've left.. at home.

7 My brother's at the cinema with .... girlfriend.

8 Has your sister got a mobile or does she use .... ?

4 Circle the correct word for each space and complete the text.

I really made a fool of (1) .... last week. My best friend and I see (2) .... every weekend, and last Saturday we went to the cinema. We bought (3) .... a drink, and then went in and sat down. A few minutes later, a woman came in and sat down next to (4) ....

Five minutes into the film, a mobile started to ring. To my horror, it was (5) .... ! This was only the start! I bent down in the dark to pick up (6) .... bag so that I could switch off the phone. Just then the woman turned to (7) .... , and said, 'What do you think you're doing?' I looked down and realised that the bag was (8) .... ! I was so embarrassed!

1 me	my	myself	mine
2 us	each other	ourselves	her
3 it	ourselves	us	them
4 her	herself	each other	us
5 myself	mine	me	my
6 my	his	mine	your
7 herself	me	her	myself
8 mine	hers	my	her

5 Are the sentences right or wrong? Correct those which are wrong.

1 I will talk to they as soon as possible. ....

2 My parents understand themselves. ....

3 There weren't much people at the party. ....

4 We looked at ourselves in the mirror. ....

5 My sister and me saw the film. ....

6 The dog is eating it's food. ....

7 My friends and I send each other emails. ....

8 Did your mum enjoy himself at the party? ....

29

16 Something, anything, nothing or everything?

1 Tick the correct sentence in each pair.

1 a She ate nothing for two days.
  b She ate anything for two days.
2 a I won't see something like it again!
  b I won't see anything like it again!

We use *something* and *nothing* in positive statements:
*I wanted to watch **something** on TV.*
*When I lost my money, there was **nothing** I could do.*

We use *anything* in negative statements and questions:
*When I lost my money, there was**n't anything** I could do (not ~~there wasn't nothing~~)*
*I could**n't** afford **anything** very expensive. (not ~~I couldn't afford something~~)*
*Did you buy **anything** to wear for the party?*
*I'm not very lucky – I **never** win **anything**.*

We also use *anything* with *will, could* and *would* to mean 'any thing, it does not matter what':
*I will do **anything** to have my watch back.*
*I liked the belt because I could wear it with **anything**.*

We use *everything* to mean 'all things':
*My friend and I do **everything** together. (not ~~do all together~~)*
*I can't say **everything** I want to say.*

2 Correct the mistake below.

I'm hungry. I didn't have nothing to eat for breakfast.

I'm hungry. I didn't .... to eat for breakfast.

3 Complete the sentences with *something, nothing, anything* or *everything*.

1 I wanted to buy ...... *something* ...... for the meal.
2 I'm not going to say .... about the accident.
3 Thanks for .... , and don't forget to write.
4 I've never heard .... as loud as that!
5 There's a bed in my room, but .... else.
6 The students would do .... the teacher asked.
7 I was really proud. I listened carefully and I understood .... !
8 I can't play billiards or .... like that.

Same sound, different spelling

1 Tick the correct sentence in each pair.

1 a My room is to small for me.
   b My room is too small for me.
2 a I hope to see you soon, maybe in France.
   b I hope to see you soon, may be in France.

To, *too* and *two* are homophones – they have the same pronunciation but different spelling:
*The music wasn't **too** loud and I talked **to** a lot of people, including **two** Italian girls.*

Aloud and *allowed* are homophones:
*We're not **allowed** to read **aloud** in the library.*

Other homophones are: *hole / whole, know / no, meat / meet, passed / past, right / write, their / there, wait / weight, weather / whether*

We use *maybe* (one word) to mean *perhaps*. This is different from *may be* (modal verb + infinitive without *to*). Similarly, *already* and *all ready* have different meanings. Compare:
*I want my room yellow, or **maybe** orange.*
*I am not sure, but the teacher **may be** late today.*
*When I got to the cinema, the film had **already** started.*
*The students are **all ready** to go.* (all the students are ready to go)

Note that we can say *the other* but not *an other*. We write *another* as one word:
*I will write you **another** letter soon.*

2 Correct the mistake below.

I'm very thirsty, so I'm having an other drink.

I'm very thirsty, so I'm having ....

3 Replace the underlined word or words where necessary.

1 I don't know <u>weather</u> it will rain tomorrow. ....*whether*...............
2 I stayed in London, and I visited Oxford <u>to</u>. ....
3 Anna couldn't go, so I went with <u>another</u> friend. ....
4 You could <u>may be</u> help me with my computer. ....
5 My train leaves at half <u>past</u> three. ....
6 Everyone was <u>all ready</u> working when I got to school. ....
7 Are the answers <u>write</u> or wrong? ....
8 My friends came to see me in <u>there</u> car. ....

31

18 Commonly confused nouns

1 Tick the correct sentence in each pair.

1 a I decided to stay in home.
  b I decided to stay at home.
2 a There's no space to write any more, I'm afraid.
  b There's no place to write any more, I'm afraid.

House or *home*?
We use *house* for the building, with a possessive form to say whose house it is; we use *home* for the place where the speaker (or the person the speaker is referring to) lives:
*Patrick and I stayed at **his house** overnight.*
*My brother left **home** when he was seventeen.*

We say *be / live / stay at home*, and *go / get / come / return / arrive home*:
*He was **at home** all evening. His parents **returned home** later that night.*

We say *be / stay, arrive at (someone's) house* and *go / get / come / return to (someone's) house.* Compare:
*I didn't **go home** until midnight.* and *My cousin and I **went to her house**.*
*We **arrived home** very late.* and *My friend will **arrive at our house** soon.*

Place, room or *space*?
We use *place* when we talk about a specific position or area. We use *room* or *space* when we talk in general. *Place* is countable; *room* and *space* are uncountable:
*There isn't much **space** in my bedroom. I don't have enough **room** for all my clothes.*
*This is a good **place** for my photos.*

2 Correct the mistake below.

It was very late when I ....

3 Correct the mistakes in these sentences where necessary.

1 I found my pen in home. ....*at home*............
2 There's a lot of room in my bag. ....
3 I haven't got enough place to put a computer. ....
4 Before I came back to home, I lived in London. ....
5 I don't think the chair is in the right place. ....
6 There were five bedrooms in our old home. ....
7 My bed is small and I need more place to sleep. ....
8 The letter arrived to our house by mistake. ....

TEST 6

1 Underline the correct word.

Mel: Is there (1) *anything / nothing* interesting on at the cinema this evening?

Ruth: Yes, the new Jude Law film's on at 6.45.

Mel: I like (2) *something / everything* he's done. Do you want to see it?

Ruth: Yes, I like him (3) *too / two*.

Mel: Shall I (4) *meat / meet* you outside the cinema at 6.30?

Ruth: Well, I (5) *maybe / may be* a little late. I need (6) *anything / something* to eat before I leave.

Mel: I'll (7) *wait / weight* for you inside the foyer then. Or shall I come round to your (8) *home / house* and give you a lift?

Ruth: That would be great! Thanks!

2 Complete the sentences with homophones.

1 We .... the shops at half .... three.

2 Can you .... your name in the box on the .... ?

3 The problem is she doesn't .... when to say ....

4 The children are waiting for .... parents over ....

5 I wonder .... the .... will be nice at the weekend.

6 I'm .... tired .... play tennis today.

7 Our teacher .... us to read ....

8 The .... class helped to dig the ....

3 Insert *n't (not)* where necessary.

1 I must say anything bad about him. ....

2 There was nothing I could say. ....

3 This sauce is anything special. ....

4 You might see something you like. ....

5 There is anything to do in this town. ....

6 You should do nothing about it. ....

7 I have got anything to wear. ....

8 Please write anything you like. ....

4 Circle the correct word for each space and complete the text.

I work with a woman who would do (1) .... for her husband. On this occasion she had organised a surprise party for him and invited lots of people. We were (2) .... and waiting for him before he got (3) .... My colleague told us to find a (4) .... to hide because her husband was on his way. I opened a cupboard door and saw that there was just (5) .... for me to climb in.

When the husband arrived, this was the time to jump out and shout 'surprise'. I pushed the door, but (6) .... happened. My friend, her husband and (7) .... colleague had to help me out. I won't do (8) .... like that again!

1	anything	everything	nothing
2	already	allready	all ready
3	at home	to home	home
4	place	room	space
5	a room	room	rooms
6	anything	nothing	something
7	an other	another	the other
8	anything	everything	something

5 Are the sentences right or wrong? Correct those which are wrong.

1 I would do everything to see my favourite actor. ....

2 When will you get at home? ....

3 My neck is very sore. ....

4 Are you OK? Is all alright? ....

5 Look! That home is for sale. ....

6 I never buy something when I go shopping. ....

7 I'm so hungry I'll eat anything you've got. ....

8 There isn't much place for all my books. ....

34

Which verbs take *to* + verb after them?

1 Tick the correct sentence in each pair.

1 a During my holiday I only want relax.
   b During my holiday I only want to relax.
2 a I would like to describe my house to you.
   b I would like describe my house to you.

We use *to* + verb after *want*:
*I **want to buy** a new radio.*

We use *to* + verb after *would like* (or *'d like*):
*Perhaps you **would like to go** for a walk.*

We also use *to* after *would love, would hate* and *would prefer*:
*I **would love to improve** my English.*

We can use either *to* + verb or verb + *-ing* after *like, love, hate* and *prefer*:
*I **like to brush** my hair in front of the mirror.* (or *I **like brushing***)

We also use *to* + verb after verbs such as *decide, expect, forget, hope, learn, need, plan, promise, try*:
*Where did you **decide to go** at the weekend?*
☆ We can also use nouns or noun phrases after all these verbs:
*I **want a new radio**.*
*I'll **decide what to do** very soon.*

2 Correct the mistake below.

I want be the best in the class!

I .... in the class!

3 Underline the correct form. In some sentences both forms are correct.

1 I'd like *go* / <u>*to go*</u> with you to the shops.
2 My sister's room is white, but she wants *painting* / *to paint* it.
3 I like *sitting* / *to sit* at the back of the class.
4 Would you like *using* / *to use* my pen?
5 I promised *help* / *to help* my friend with her homework.
6 My friends love *dancing* / *to dance*, but I don't.
7 You know I want *see* / *to see* you soon.
8 I'd hate *missing* / *to miss* my plane.

Which form of the verb do I use after *look forward to*?

1 **Tick the correct sentence in each pair.**

1 a I'm looking forward to telling you the whole story.
  b I'm looking forward to tell you the whole story.
2 a I don't enjoy walking in the dark.
  b I don't enjoy walk in the dark.

We use *to* + verb after some verbs (see Unit 19):
*I **want to change** my bed because it is old.*

However, we use *look forward to* + verb + *-ing*:
*I **look forward to hearing** from you.* (not ~~I look forward to hear from you.~~)
*We're **looking forward to seeing** you soon.*

This is because *to* in *look forward to* is a preposition:
*Are you **looking forward to** the end of term?*

We use *-ing* after both the preposition *to* and other prepositions such as *in, on, for*:
*I prefer speaking **to writing** English.*
*Are you interested **in going** on the tour?*

We also use verb + *-ing* after verbs such as *avoid, enjoy, finish, practise, stop*:
*We really **enjoy being** in this class.*
*I **finished writing** my diary at half past eleven.*

2 **Correct the mistake below.**

> I'm looking forward to be with you again on the 17th.

I .... with you again on the 17th.

3 **Complete the sentences with the *to* or *-ing* form of the verb.**

1 Are you looking forward to ....*going*........ *(go)* back home?
2 I hope .... *(spend)* more time with my friends after the exams.
3 I'm keen on .... *(read)* books in English.
4 I want .... *(buy)* a new television because mine is broken.
5 Nobody is looking forward to .... *(do)* the test.
6 Thanks for .... *(help)* me with my homework.
7 I look forward to .... *(receive)* your letter.
8 I try .... *(use)* the underground as little as possible.

Which form of the verb do I use after *can* and *could*?

1 Tick the correct sentence in each pair.

  1 a I hope you can to send me a photo.
     b I hope you can send me a photo.
  2 a We went to a restaurant where we could talk in peace.
     b We went to a restaurant where we could talked in peace.

We use *can* + infinitive without *to*:
*Maybe we **can see** each other in the holidays.*
*You **can find** everything you need in the market.*

We also use the infinitive without *to* after *might, could, should, must*:
*Our teacher said she **might be** late.*
*We **could stop** now and **have** a drink.*
***Should** I **tell** you what I did?*

We use *could* + infinitive without *to* to talk about the past. We don't change the form of the main verb:
*When I entered the club, I **couldn't see** any of my friends.* (not ~~I couldn't saw~~)
*I wanted to help my friend, but there was nothing I **could do**.*

☆ Note that we use *could* + *have (done)* for things which were possible but didn't happen in the past:
*I **could have told** you the answer, but you didn't ask me.*

2 Correct the mistake below.

There are no curtains at the window, so I can to see into the street.

There are no curtains at the window, so .... into the street.

3 Underline the correct form in these sentences.

  1 The teacher can *speaks / speak* three languages.
  2 I don't think you should *touch / to touch* that button.
  3 We went to a place where we could *had / have* coffee.
  4 I'm sorry, I can't *come / to come* with you to Florida.
  5 I hoped I could *find / found* my bike quickly.
  6 I'm sure we can *meet / met* some nice people at the club.
  7 If the weather's nice, we can *swim / swimming* in the sea.
  8 We must *be / to be* on time for our lessons.

TEST 7

1 Insert *to* in these sentences where necessary.

1 Do you want read this letter? ....
2 Should I tell you what I did? ....
3 We need buy a bottle of water. ....
4 I couldn't swim until I had lessons. ....
5 I'd hate live in the country. ....
6 My friend could have waited for me. ....
7 We mustn't forget his birthday. ....
8 I'd like pass my exams. ....

2 Rewrite the sentences with the *-ing* form of the verb where possible.

1 Do you like to relax at the weekend? ....
2 I'd love to know someone famous. ....
3 My friend hates to be late for work. ....
4 Some people prefer to get up early. ....
5 I'd like to go to Canada next year. ....
6 I'd prefer to sit by the window. ....
7 I love to watch old films on TV. ....
8 I'd hate to break my leg. ....

3 Complete the sentences with suitable verbs.

1
I prefer playing football to
.... it on TV.

5
I'm looking forward to
.... my
friend at the weekend.

2
You mustn't ....
on that seat.

6
You could ....
the exam, but you didn't work
very hard.

3
Some people avoid
....
their homework.

7
I'm afraid I don't know where
your pen is. I'm sorry for
.... it.

4
Would you like ....
to the cinema?

8
May I borrow your ruler? I
forgot ....
mine with me.

4 Circle the correct word for each space and complete the text.

David: I.thought we might (1).. out for a meal on Saturday.
         Would you like (2) .... that?

Jane: I'm not sure. It's my sister's birthday and I promised (3) ....
         her in town. I need (4) .... her a present.

David: What are you planning (5) .... her?

Jane: A CD perhaps. She enjoys (6) .... to music.

David: What about the latest Robbie Williams CD?

Jane: Oh, no. She stopped (7) .... to pop music a long time ago.
         She prefers classical music now.

David: Perhaps the three of us could (8) .... lunch together.

Jane: That sounds like a good idea.

1 go	going	to go
2 do	doing	to do
3 meet	meeting	to meet
4 buy	buying	to buy
5 get	getting	to get
6 listen	listening	to listen
7 listen	listening	to listen
8 have	having	to have

5 Are the sentences right or wrong? Correct those which are wrong.

1 Are you looking forward going home? ....

2 I'd like to pass the PET exam. ....

3 Should I to tell you what I did? ....

4 I enjoy to look at other people's photos. ....

5 I went shopping earlier. I could buy some milk. ....

6 It was late, so I wanted go home. ....

7 My brother is keen on running. ....

8 I couldn't spoke English two years ago. ....

How do I form adjectives from nouns?

1 Tick the correct sentence in each pair.

1   a   It's a sunny day today in Spain.
     b   It's a sun day today in Spain.
2   a   I hope my sister will be surprise when she opens her present.
     b   I hope my sister will be surprised when she opens her present.

Adjectives are sometimes formed by adding *-y, -al*, etc. to the noun:
*There was a lot of **rain**. → It was very **rainy**.*

Here are some more adjective endings:

- *-al*: *environment → environmental, music → musical*
- *-ful*: *colour → colourful, wonder → wonderful*
- *-less* (meaning 'without'): *child → childless, home → homeless*
- *-ish*: *fool → foolish, self → selfish*
- *-ous*: *danger → dangerous, mountain → mountainous*

Sometimes we have to change the ending of the noun to form the adjective:
sun → sunny, beauty → beautiful, fame → famous

Many adjectives end in *-ed* and *-ing*. Adjectives ending in *-ed* describe how people feel and adjectives ending in *-ing* cause people to feel this way. For example:
*I'm **interested** in this book.* and ***This book** looks **interesting**.*
*I wasn't **surprised** I missed the plane.* and *It wasn't **surprising** I missed the plane.*

2 Correct the mistake below.

I was really shocking when I saw my hair.

I .... when I saw my hair.

3 Complete the sentences with the adjective form.

1   If you ride your bike at night, it can be .... dangerous .... *(danger)*.
2   My parents bought me a .... *(wonder)* present for my birthday.
3   My friends aren't .... *(interest)* in classical music.
4   I don't like peanuts and crisps – they're too .... *(salt)*.
5   There's a .... *(disgust)* smell outside my building. It's awful!
6   It's cold and .... *(cloud)* today.
7   I was really .... *(surprise)* to see my brother.
8   Sometimes I'm a bit .... *(care)* and I make too many mistakes.

Very or really?

1 Tick the correct sentence in each pair.

  1 a The weather was very awful on Saturday.
     b The weather was really awful on Saturday.
  2 a I'm sure the party will be very funny.
     b I'm sure the party will be great fun.

We use *very* with adjectives such as *big* and *angry*. The words *huge* and *furious* mean 'very big' and 'very angry', so we use adverbs such as *absolutely* and *completely* instead:
*I thought the palace would be **very big**, but it was **absolutely huge**.*
☆ We do not use *so*, *much* or *too* instead of *very* in the above sentence.

We use *really* with *big / huge* and other pairs of adjectives. Compare:
***very / really** good* and ***really / absolutely** excellent, fantastic, great, wonderful*
***very / really** bad* and ***really / absolutely** awful, dreadful, horrible, terrible*

We can use *very* with *much*, but this is usually in negative sentences:
*I don't like opera **very much**, but I like modern music **a lot**.*

If something makes us laugh, we say it is *(very) funny*. But if we're enjoying ourselves, we say we're having *(great) fun*. A person can also be *(great) fun*:
*My cousin is **great fun**. He tells some **very funny** stories.*

2 Correct the mistake below.

The film was very fantastic. I watched it three times.

The film .... I watched it three times.

3 Add *very* or *really* to these sentences. In some sentences both words are possible.

  1 We had a great time at the weekend. ....*really great*............
  2 When I got into the bath, the water was cold. ....
  3 I had a good time on Saturday evening. ....
  4 My sister didn't say much when we saw each other. ....
  5 My bedroom isn't enormous. ....
  6 It wasn't funny when I lost my keys. ....
  7 Learning English is important to me. ....
  8 I thought the jokes were hilarious. ....

24 How do I form adverbs?

1 Tick the correct sentence in each pair.

1 a When I heard the news, I left *immediately*.
  b When I heard the news, I left *immediatly*.
2 a I was *really* tired when I got home.
  b I was *realy* tired when I got home.

We use adverbs to describe verbs. In general, we form an adverb by adding *-ly* to an adjective:

clear → clearly, fortunate → fortunately, careful → carefully

If an adjective ends in *y*, we change the *y* to *i* before adding *-ly*:

easy → easily, happy → happily, lucky → luckily

We can't make adverbs from adjectives such as *friendly* and *lovely*, which already end in *-ly*. Instead we use the adjective + *fashion, manner* or *way*:

*The teacher spoke to me **in a friendly way**.*

Some adverbs are irregular. *Good* is an adjective and *well* is an adverb; *fast* and *hard* are both. We also use *hardly* before a verb to mean 'only just, almost not':

*I **hardly play** chess at all. My brother is a **good** chess **player**. He **plays** chess **well**. He **works hard** to improve his game.*

We sometimes use adverbs such as *really, completely, absolutely, truly (true + -ly)* with adjectives (see Unit 23):

*My new watch is **truly lovely**.*

2 Correct the mistake below.

I'm particulary pleased with the card from my sister.

I'm .... with the card from my sister.

3 Complete the sentences with the adverb form.

1 The room was ....*completely*......... *(complete)* empty when I went in.
2 And .... *(final)*, I would like to thank everyone for coming.
3 I am .... *(true)* sorry for what happened.
4 I look forward to hearing from you. Yours .... *(sincere)*, Jess Cripps.
5 The other team wasn't very good, so we won .... *(easy)*.
6 My friend is .... *(definite)* the best student in the class.
7 My father drove very .... *(fast)*, so we got there on time.
8 I was late for school, but .... *(lucky)* the teacher was late too.

1 **Underline the adverbs and circle the adjectives in this text.**

One day my sister saw a truly lovely mug when we were out shopping. She bent down and picked up the mug to look at the price on the bottom. As she did this, lots of tea splashed down the front of her T-shirt! I had to try hard not to laugh at her shocked face! My sister wanted to get out of the shop as fast as she could, but an assistant came over to us. It turned out to be her mug, which she'd left on the shelf by mistake. The assistant was clearly as embarrassed as my sister, but I just thought it was funny!

2 **Add the word in brackets.**

1 I didn't do well in my exam. *(very)*

   ....

2 Our homework wasn't hard – it was impossible! *(completely)*

   ....

3 I'm interested in Italian architecture. *(very)*

   ....

4 The acting was awful and the story was bad too. *(very)*

   ....

5 We enjoy our lessons because the teacher is fun. *(great)*

   ....

6 My handwriting is bad. *(really)*

   ....

7 Do you go out much? *(very)*

   ....

8 Jim Carrey's funny, isn't he? *(really)*

   ....

3 Complete the rest of the missing words.

1 My sister can be *self*.................... .
2 *Luck*...................... , I got there on time.
3 Can you play a *music*...................... instrument?
4 I asked him to drive more *care*...................... .
5 We stood up *quick*...................... .
6 I'm not *interest*...................... in science fiction.
7 It was wet and *wind*...................... yesterday.
8 Your sister is a *love*...................... person.

4 Complete the second sentence so that it has the same meaning as the first.

1 I thought the holiday was very disappointing.
I was .... the holiday.
2 There was a lot of snow at the weekend.
It was .... the weekend.
3 The lesson was boring for us.
We .... the lesson.
4 I hardly watch television at all.
I don't .... television.
5 This is a wonderful book.
This book ....
6 There are a lot of mountains in that area.
That area ....
7 He plays the flute beautifully.
He's ....
8 She's a very fast driver.
She drives ....

5 Are the sentences right or wrong? Correct those which are wrong.

1 I was pleasing with my new jeans. ....
2 Italian food is really great! ....
3 Some students work hardly at all. ....
4 I'm sure the party will be funny. ....
5 The views from my window are wonder. ....
6 I foolishly forgot to lock the door. ....
7 I did my homework quite easyly. ....
8 The weather was lovely truly. ....

Which, who or that?

1 Tick the correct sentence in each pair.

1 a I have found a cupboard who looks nice in my room.

   b I have found a cupboard which looks nice in my room.

2 a My teacher is a person likes speaking other languages.

   b My teacher is a person who likes speaking other languages.

We use *which* for things and *who* for people when we combine two pieces of information to say exactly which thing or person. *Which* and *who* refer to the subject:
*I'm wearing **a ring**. **It** was my aunt's.* → *I'm wearing **a ring which** was my aunt's.*
*I know **a woman**. **She** is a doctor.* → *I know **a woman who** is a doctor.*
***The waiter** was Italian. **He** served us.* → ***The waiter who** served us was Italian.*

We can use *that* instead of *which* or *who* in sentences like these, although *who* is more common for people (especially family members). We don't usually use *that* for people.

We often use *which / that* and *who* when we define things or people. We don't use *what*:
*A dictionary is a book **which / that** lists words and tells you what they mean. (not a book **what** lists)*
*A waiter is someone **who** serves customers food and drink.*

We can either include or omit *which*, *who* and *that* when they refer to the object:
*The teacher told **a joke**. I already knew **it**.* → *The teacher told **a joke (which / that)** I already knew.*

Depending on the emphasis you want to give, you could also say:
*I already knew **the joke (which / that)** the teacher told.*

2 Correct the mistake below.

I have an alarm clock who wakes me up.

I have .... me up.

3 Add *who* or *which* to these sentences where necessary.

1 I've got a key doesn't work very well. ...*a key which doesn't work*...

2 I wore the dress I bought on Saturday. ....

3 Tick the sentences are correct. ....

4 My dad had a cousin lives in South Africa. ....

5 Where is the chair is broken? ....

6 My mother is someone you can talk to about anything. ....

7 I don't know anyone works in a hospital. ....

8 A machine washes dishes is called a dishwasher. ....

45

How do I give extra information?

1 Tick the correct sentence in each pair.

1 a This ring, which my boyfriend bought for my birthday, is very special to me.
  b This ring, that my boyfriend bought for my birthday, is very special to me.
2 a We went home by bus, that was a good decision.
  b We went home by bus, which was a good decision.

We use *which* to give extra information about something:
*The walls, **which** are pink, need painting again.*
*I'm in Brazil, **which** is a beautiful country.*
☆ We use a comma before and after the extra information when it comes in the middle of a sentence, and before the extra information when it comes at the end.

In the same way, we use *who* to give extra information about someone:
*My best friend, **who** is the same age as I am, wants to study English too.*

We don't use *that* to give extra information:
*My room, **which** is on the first floor, is very small.* (not *My room, that is on the first floor*)
*I work with Emilia, **who** comes from Peru.* (not *Emilia, that comes from Peru*)

When we talk about 'a fact', we use *which*:
*I failed my exam, **which** was surprising.* (not *my exam, **that** was surprising*)

We use *what* to mean 'the things that'. Compare:
*That is the information **which / that** I have.* and *That is the information I have.*
(not *the information what I have*)
*I can tell you **what** I know.*

2 Correct the mistake below.

I have to do the ironing, that is really boring.

I have to do the ironing, ... boring.

3 Underline the correct word and add commas where necessary.

1 The lamp, *that / which* doesn't work very well, is next to my bed.
2 I stayed in the Marriot Hotel *that / which* was very nice.
3 I didn't understand *what / which* the teacher said.
4 I work with three people *who / which* are my age.
5 Tübingen *that / which* is a really good team will probably win the match.
6 You can come with me *what / which* would be great.
7 I have everything *that / what* I need.
8 My teacher *that / who* is very nice reminds me of my cousin.

46

Which prepositions do I use after *arrive*?

1 Tick the correct sentence in each pair.

1 a I arrived at my hotel an hour ago.
  b I arrived to my hotel an hour ago.
2 a I'm going to arrive in the afternoon.
  b I'm going to arrive at the afternoon.

We say *arrive in* a country, city or town and *arrive at* all other places:
*I have just **arrived in** Brazil.*
*We **arrived at** the airport two hours before our flight.*

In informal situations we can use *get (to)* instead of *arrive (in / at)*. We also say *arrive home / get home, arrive here / get here* and *arrive there / get there*:
*We will **arrive in Malaga** very soon.* and *We will **get to Malaga** very soon.*
*I didn't **arrive at work** until ten o'clock.* and *I didn't **get to work** until ten o'clock.*
*We **arrived home late at night**.* and *We **got home late at night**.*
☆ Note that you can *arrive*, but you must *get somewhere*:
*I'll phone you when we **arrive**.* (not ~~when we get~~)

We use *at, in* and *on* with expressions of time:
- at: ***at** two o'clock, **at** midnight, **at** night, **at** the weekend, **at** Christmas*
- in: ***in** the evening, **in** July, **in** summer, **in** 2008*
- on: ***on** Monday, **on** Monday evening, **on** 22 July, **on** Christmas Day*
☆ Note that we usually talk about place before time:
*I arrived **at school at half past eight** in the morning.*

2 Correct the mistake below.

When I .... , the train was just leaving.

3 Tick (✓) the sentences which are correct. In some pairs both sentences are correct.

1 a Alice will get there soon. ......✓...... b Alice will arrive there soon. ......✓......
2 a I got at the club at eight. .... b I arrived at the club at eight ....
3 a They got home last week. .... b They arrived home last week. ....
4 a He often gets to school late. .... b He often arrives to school late. ....
5 a What time will you get? .... b What time will you arrive? ....
6 a When do you get in Paris? .... b When did you arrive in Paris? ....
7 a We got to Spain safely. .... b We arrived to Spain safely. ....
8 a I'm sure he'll get here soon. .... b I'm sure he'll arrive here soon. ....

TEST 9

1 Complete the sentences with an appropriate preposition where necessary.

1 We're staying with my parents .... the weekend.

2 My parents should arrive .... very soon.

3 I got .... school early this morning.

4 We arrived .... New Zealand late at night.

5 What time will you get .... here?

6 My sister's baby arrived .... Monday.

7 When the team arrived .... the ground, the gates were locked.

8 My friends and I sometimes eat out .... the evening.

2 Insert commas where necessary.

1 This CD which you can borrow if you like is really great! ....

2 I'm reading a book which my sister lent me. ....

3 A penknife is a knife which folds into a case. ....

4 Miranda who's an art teacher is a great painter. ....

5 I don't know what you mean. ....

6 Can you see Dr Jones who I was talking to? ....

7 The woman who works with me is from Milan. ....

8 Our train arrived on time which was amazing! ....

3 Join the pairs of sentences. Use commas where necessary.

1 Swimming is good fun. It's good exercise too.

....

2 Agatha Christie was British. She was born in 1890.

....

3 The boy is wearing glasses. He can't see very well.

....

4 Jane sent me an email. It was full of news.

....

5 The teacher taught us. She explained the grammar rules clearly.

....

6 My mum has got a mobile. She phones me every day.

....

7 My friend sent me a postcard. It was nice of her.

....

8 Look at these pens. I bought them.

....

4 Circle the correct word for each space and complete the text.

John Brown is a London taxi driver (1) .... loves going to the theatre.
Last week his mum gave him two tickets for a play, (2) .... was very
kind of her. The tickets were for Wednesday evening. Then John read some reviews of
the play, (3) .... all said it was awful! He didn't want to see a play
(4) .... no-one liked, but what should he do with the tickets?

Two hours before the play started (5) .... Wednesday evening, he left
the tickets on the back seat of his taxi. Perhaps someone (6) ....
wanted to see the play would take them. However, when John finished work
(7) .... eleven o'clock that night, the tickets
were still there. In fact, there were now four tickets on the
seat! Someone had placed another pair of tickets on top of
them! John still doesn't know (8) ....
he's going to say to his mum!

1	that	which	who
2	that	what	which
3	what	which	who
4	that	what	who
5	at	in	on
6	what	which	who
7	at	in	on
8	that	what	which

5 Are the sentences right or wrong? Correct those which are wrong.

1 My gran, who's nearly 80 is learning French. ....
2 I've got a pen who doesn't write very well. ....
3 Let me know when you get to there. ....
4 I know someone, who comes from Alicante. ....
5 My friend watched a video that I'd already seen it ....
6 Have you done the homework we got yesterday? ....
7 We arrived to Japan last week. ....
8 My sister listened very carefully, that was unusual. ....

49

28 Commonly confused verbs

1 Tick the correct sentence in each pair.

1 a My friends asked me to come to the cinema with them.
  b My friends asked me to go to the cinema with them.
2 a I lived in Nice for two weeks last summer.
  b I stayed in Nice for two weeks last summer.

Come or *go*?
We use *come* to talk about moving towards the person who is speaking or the place they are talking about. We use *go* to talk about moving from one place to another. We often say *come / go back* to mean *return* and we always say *come here* and *go there*:
*I'm having a lovely time here in Cambridge, so I hope to **come back** one day.*
*I can't find my purse, so I'm going to **go back** to the cinema.*

Bring or *take*?
We use *bring* when we come to a place with something (or someone) and *take* when we go to a place with something (or someone):
*When I **come** to your party, I'll **bring** a cake. But if I **go** to Suzy's party, I won't **take** one.*

Live or *stay*?
We use *live* when we talk about our home. We use *stay* when we talk about being somewhere as a visitor or a guest, often for a short time. We also use *stay* to talk about continuing to be at a place without going away:
*I **live** with my parents. We're going to **stay** in a hotel while our flat is being decorated.*
*The disco was great, so we decidied to **stay** there all evening.*

2 Correct the mistake below.

New York was great!
I'd love to come back
there next year.

New York was great! I .... there next year.

3 Complete the sentences with a verb from this page.

1 My friend told me about the concert tomorrow. I think I'll ....go............ too.
2 My friends don't usually .... to my house.
3 Do you .... in a house or a flat?
4 On Sundays I usually .... in bed until midday.
5 Don't forget to .... your camera when you go on the trip.
6 You can .... with my family when you come here.
7 I left my jacket at the restaurant, so I had to .... back later.
8 Can I .... my sister to your party?

How do I use *do* and *go* with *-ing* words?

1 **Tick the correct sentence in each pair.**

1 a I did some shopping for the weekend on my way home.
    b I did shopping for the weekend on my way home.
2 a I go swimming at my local pool.
    b I do swimming at my local pool.

We say *go shopping* when we refer to the activity of shopping in general. We can also say *go shopping for*:
*I love to **go shopping** at the weekend.* (not *I love to **go for** shopping*)
*My boyfriend went to a football match and I **went shopping**.*
*I usually **go shopping for** souvenirs when I'm on holiday.*

We say *do the shopping* (or *my / some shopping*) when we refer to shopping for specific things:
*My parents are coming for dinner tonight. I must **do the shopping** at lunchtime.*

In the same way, we say *do the washing, do the washing up, do the ironing, do the cleaning, do the cooking.*

We also use *go* with sports which end in *-ing*: *go running, go skiing, go swimming*, etc.
☆ Note that we use *been* as the past participle of *go* when we talk about our experiences:
*I like to **go jogging** three times a week.*
*I've never **been sailing**.* (not *I've never **gone sailing**.*)

2 **Correct the mistake below.**

I prefer to do shopping for clothes on my own.

I prefer .... on my own.

3 **Underline the correct form.**

1 I sometimes <u>go shopping</u> / go for shopping with my best friend.
2 My friend *does running / goes running* every morning.
3 I've *been swimming / gone swimming* in the river.
4 My brother *did diving / went diving* for the first time last year.
5 I bought some water when I was *doing the shopping / going shopping.*
6 I've never *been shopping / done shopping* in New York.
7 I *do cooking / do the cooking* when I get home from work.
8 We *do skiing / go skiing* in the mountains every year.

Which verbs take *to* (preposition) after them?

1 Tick the correct sentence in each pair.

1 a I explained to my friend how the Internet works.
  b I explained my friend how the Internet works.
2 a My mother told me that I should be careful.
  b My mother said me that I should be careful.

We use the preposition *to* with the following verbs:
- *listen, write, explain, speak, talk, say to (someone)*:
  *Please **write to** me soon.*
  *I **speak to** my boyfriend every day.*
- *explain, write, send, describe (something) to (someone)*:
  *I'll **explain** the problem **to** you when I see you.*
- *listen to (something)*:
  *I bought a CD player so that I could **listen to** music.*
- *invite (someone) to (something)*:
  *I'm going to **invite** my friends **to** the party.*

We don't use the preposition *to* with the following verbs:
- *telephone, tell, ask (someone)*:
  *I didn't **telephone** my parents because I couldn't find my mobile.*
- *write, send, ask (someone something)*:
  *My mother didn't **send** me a postcard from Sicily.*

2 Correct the mistake below.

I like listening my cassettes and CDs.

I .... and CDs.

3 Add *to* to these sentences where necessary.

1 The man explained me who he was. ......*explained to me*......
2 I'll write you again when I feel better. ....
3 I wrote my sister a long letter. ....
4 My friend invited me dinner in a restaurant. ....
5 Sometimes I send text messages my friends. ....
6 Tell me about your holiday in Spain. ....
7 I often ask the teacher questions. ....
8 The teacher said goodbye us. ....

1 Underline the correct form.

1 I'm going to *bring* / *take* my digital camera back to the shop.
2 I'll probably *live* / *stay* with my parents until I get married.
3 Please *come* / *go* here quickly!
4 I'm going to *live* / *stay* at my grandparents' tonight.
5 Some people *do* / *go* shopping every day.
6 I don't want to *say* / *talk* to you.
7 We *lived* / *stayed* in a small apartment when we were on holiday.
8 The teacher *said* / *told* us to listen carefully.

2 Complete the sentences with the word in brackets and the correct form of *do* or *go*. Use *the* where necessary.

On her way home from work Sally always goes to the supermarket and
(1) .... *(shopping)*. After that she (2) ....
(cooking) and the washing up. This evening Sally's watching TV –
she's watching a holiday programme about Thailand! Sally would love
to go to Thailand! She'd love to lie on the beautiful beaches and
(3) .... *(swimming)* in the warm blue sea. She'd love to
(4) .... *(kayaking)* around the small islands. Perhaps
she could (5) .... *(sailing)* too. She's never
(6) .... *(diving)*, so she'd also like to try that. She'd also
like to (7) .... *(shopping)* for souvenirs and presents!
But for Sally, Thailand is only a dream. While she's watching TV, she's
(8) .... *(ironing)*!

3 Tick (✓) the sentences which are correct. In some pairs both sentences are correct.

  1 a She said she'd phone me. ....   b She said she'd phone to me. ....
→ 2 a Will you write me a letter? ....   b Will you write a letter to me? ....
  3 a I can describe you the picture. .... b I can describe the picture to you. ....
  4 a Do you like listening the radio? .... b Do you like listening to the radio? ....
  5 a I'll speak you soon. ....   b I'll speak to you soon. ....
  6 a The teacher told us her name. ....   b The teacher told to us her name. ....
➥ 7 a I sent my parents a postcard. ....   b I sent a postcard to my parents. ....
  8 a This is what she said me. ....   b This is what she said to me. ....

4 Complete each sentence with a word from the box. Sometimes more than one word is possible.

ask	say	send	speak	tell	write

  1 I'll .... to you soon.
  2 Let's .... the teacher what we think.
  3 He didn't .... me to do it.
  4 When will you .... the parcel to me?
  5 I couldn't .... anything to them.
  6 I'm going to .... some postcards.
  7 I'll .... it only to you.
  8 I want to .... you a question.

5 Are the sentences right or wrong? Correct those which are wrong.

  1 How often do you go for shopping? ....
  2 I'll write you soon. ....
  3 Can you bring me a present from London? ....
  4 My friend invited me her house. ....
  5 I'd like to stay abroad one day. ....
  6 I didn't want to come there. ....
  7 Why don't you telephone to me? ....
  8 My sister does jogging twice a week. ....

Answer key

Unit 1
1 1 a
    2 b
2 a white van
3 2 a / one
    3 a
    4 a
    5 one
    6 an
    7 a
    8 an / one

Unit 2
1 1 b
    2 a
2 a dentist's appointment on Tuesday
3 2 London is on the Thames.
    3 Are you learning Italian?
    4 My father is Spanish.
    5 I don't like Mondays.
    6 My birthday is in May.
    7 Yours faithfully, Paul May
    8 My mum is a doctor.

Unit 3
1 1 a
    2 a
2 I'm going to clean
3 2 it is / it's too small
    3 Here are our photos.
    4 and is married to Anna
    5 which are interesting
    6 That is / That's all for now.
    7 I am / I'm looking forward
    8 Jack is / Jack's afraid

Test 1
1 1 an exam, a hard exam
    2 a university, an old university
    3 an idea, an interesting idea
    4 a house, an unusual house
    5 a restaurant, an expensive restaurant
    6 an hour, an extra hour
    7 an uncle, a rich uncle
    8 a lesson, an easy lesson

2 Sandfield Road; Oxford; OX3 7RN; February; Dear Mrs Brown; Please find; March 15th; My husband and I; Yours sincerely; Barbara Parker
3 1 is / 's
    2 am / 'm
    3 am / 'm
    4 are
    5 is / 's
    6 are
    7 is / 's
    8 is / 's
4 1 The Nile is the longest river in Africa.
    2 Chinese New Year is often in January.
    3 Nicole Kidman is an Australian actress.
    4 Juventus and Lazio are Italian football teams.
    5 King Lear is a play about an old English king and his three daughters.
    6 The Himalayas are in Asia.
    7 Shops in Britain are often open on Sunday.
    8 Los Angeles is in California.
5 1 the Pacific Ocean
    2 a friend of mine
    3 They're / They are not sure
    4 *correct*
    5 There are some people
    6 I'm / I am very tired
    7 *correct*
    8 in half an hour

Unit 4
1 1 a
    2 b
2 an old carpet and curtains
3 2 holidays
    3 mountain
    4 cloth
    5 curtains
    6 holiday
    7 clothes
    8 mountains

Unit 5

1 1 a

2 a

2 There's some money

3 2 are

3 was

4 are

5 woman

6 hair looks

7 slices of bread

8 was

Unit 6

1 1 a

2 a

2 my mother's best friend

3 2 her family's other house

3 the name of his company

4 my little brother's birthday

5 My father's cousins

6 my best friend's brothers

7 My friends' phone numbers

8 the man's glasses

Test 2

1 1 baby's

2 wife's

3 *not necessary*

4 friends'

5 *not necessary*

6 teacher's

7 boy's

8 children's

2 1 *not necessary*

2 *not necessary*

3 curtains

4 officers

5 *not necessary*

6 mountains

7 *not necessary*

8 cloths

3 1 are the men's books

2 furniture in the bedrooms is quite old

3 books are on the desks

4 you know those women over there

5 those your friends' jackets

6 boys are doing their homework

7 new cars are quite nice

8 children wear glasses

4 1 some tea

I'd like a cup of tea.

2 some cake

Can I have a piece of cake?

3 some chocolate

Would you like a bar of chocolate?

4 some water

Could I have a glass of water?

5 some jam

Do you want a jar of jam?

6 some lemonade

Shall I get a bottle of lemonade?

7 some bread

Did you buy a loaf of bread?

8 some sugar

I'm going to buy a packet of sugar.

5 1 Which clothes

2 some information

3 *correct*

4 There is some food

5 *correct*

6 I eat some fruit

7 at the front of the class

8 my grandparents' car

Unit 7

1 1 a

2 b

2 didn't have a TV

3 2 b

3 a

4 *both*

5 a

6 *both*

7 b

8 *both*

Unit 8

1 1 b

2 b

2 I'm not eating very much

3 2 wear

3 'm / am reading

4 play

5 'm / am wearing

6 reads

7 's / is playing
8 'm / am working

Unit 9
1 1 a
   2 a
2 smells of
3 2 b
   3 *both*
   4 b
   5 a
   6 b
   7 *both*
   8 b

Test 3
1 1 hasn't got / doesn't have
   2 haven't got / don't have
   3 didn't have
   4 won't have
   5 hasn't got / doesn't have
   6 don't have
   7 doesn't have / hasn't got
   8 didn't have
2 1 'm trying
   2 'm making
   3 goes
   4 tastes
   5 'm reading
   6 don't go
   7 have
   8 is improving
3 1 's trying, doesn't want
   2 'm not enjoying, want
   3 needs, 's using
   4 play, don't like
   5 'm thinking, believe
   6 'm watching, don't make
   7 're wearing, smells
   8 's having, think
4 1 'm having / am having
   2 'm staying / am staying
   3 's working / is working
   4 can see
   5 go
   6 'm sitting / am sitting
   7 can hear
   8 know

5 1 *correct*
   2 We always have a party
   3 I don't need
   4 Birds make
   5 didn't have
   6 *correct*
   7 I'm wearing
   8 We think

Unit 10
1 1 a
   2 b
2 found them
3 2 said
   3 cut
   4 lived
   5 brought
   6 stayed
   7 bought
   8 studied

Unit 11
1 1 a
   2 b
2 because he didn't sleep well
3 2 didn't play
   3 didn't stay
   4 didn't tell
   5 didn't hear
   6 didn't get married
   7 didn't expect
   8 didn't return

Unit 12
1 1 b
   2 a
2 was going out when the phone rang
3 2 broke
   3 went
   4 was doing
   5 bought
   6 was sitting
   7 didn't understand
   8 won

Test 4

1
1 got
2 watched
3 made
4 put
5 read
6 did
7 felt
8 went

2
1 didn't take
2 didn't cost
3 didn't have
4 didn't find
5 didn't feel
6 didn't want
7 didn't know
8 didn't get

3
1 didn't play
2 listened
3 didn't meet
4 didn't get up
5 washed
6 didn't write
7 didn't do
8 didn't go

4
1 drove
2 were standing
3 was sitting
4 switched
5 was living
6 put
7 was wearing
8 went

5
1 didn't have a car
2 fell out of bed
3 *correct*
4 didn't stay long
5 We started
6 *correct*
7 was skiing in Italy
8 I bought

Unit 13

1
1 b
2 b

2 with me

3
2 hers
3 us

4 her
5 them
6 him
7 mine
8 ours

Unit 14

1
1 a
2 a

2 don't like each other

3
2 each other
3 herself
4 myself
5 us
6 each other
7 yourselves
8 themselves

Unit 15

1
1 b
2 b

2 a lot of work to do before I go

3 *In some cases both sentences are acceptable, but one is regarded as correct in formal or written English (indicated in brackets).*
2 *both* (b)
3 *both* (b)
4 a
5 *both* (b)
6 a
7 *both* (b)
8 *both* (b)

Test 5

1
1 I don't do much homework.
2 I haven't got many clothes.
3 I don't do much sport.
4 I don't work with many people.
5 I don't know much about football.
6 I don't go to the theatre much.
7 I don't watch many videos.
8 I don't eat much pasta.

2
1 I can show him to his classroom.
2 I don't want much for lunch.
3 She stood up and introduced herself.
4 You can use my pen or yours.

5 They didn't like her very much.
6 She had a surprise for them.
7 Our stories are the most interesting.
8 I did a lot at the weekend.

3 1 your
2 ours
3 her
4 theirs
5 our
6 mine
7 his
8 yours

4 1 myself
2 each other
3 ourselves
4 us
5 mine
6 my
7 me
8 hers

5 1 talk to them
2 understand each other
3 many people
4 *correct*
5 My sister and I saw
6 eating its food
7 *correct*
8 enjoy herself

Unit 16
1 1 a
2 b
2 have anything
3 2 anything
3 everything
4 anything
5 nothing
6 anything
7 everything
8 anything

Unit 17
1 1 b
2 a
2 another drink
3 2 too
3 *not necessary*
4 maybe

5 *not necessary*
6 already
7 right
8 their

Unit 18
1 1 b
2 a
2 came back home
3 2 *not necessary*
3 enough space / room
4 came back home
5 *not necessary*
6 our old house
7 more space / room
8 at our house

Test 6
1 1 anything
2 everything
3 too
4 meet
5 may be
6 something
7 wait
8 house
2 1 passed, past
2 write, right
3 know, no
4 their, there
5 whether, weather
6 too, to
7 allowed, aloud
8 whole, hole
3 1 mustn't say
2 *not necessary*
3 isn't anything
4 *not necessary*
5 isn't anything
6 *not necessary*
7 haven't got
8 *not necessary*
4 1 anything
2 all ready
3 home
4 place
5 room
6 nothing

7 another
8 anything
5 1 do anything
2 get home
3 *correct*
4 everything all right
5 That house
6 buy anything
7 *correct*
8 space *or* room

Unit 19
1 1 b
2 a
2 want to be the best
3 2 to paint
3 *both*
4 to use
5 to help
6 *both*
7 to see
8 to miss

Unit 20
1 1 a
2 a
2 'm looking forward to being
3 2 to spend
3 reading
4 to buy
5 doing
6 helping
7 receiving
8 to use

Unit 21
1 1 b
2 a
2 I can see
3 2 touch
3 have
4 come
5 find
6 meet
7 swim
8 be

Test 7
1 1 want to read
2 *not necessary*
3 need to buy
4 *not necessary*
5 hate to live
6 *not necessary*
7 *not necessary*
8 like to pass
2 1 Do you like relaxing at the weekend?
2 *not possible*
3 My friend hates being late for work.
4 Some people prefer getting up early.
5 *not possible*
6 *not possible*
7 I love watching old films on TV.
8 *not possible*
3 1 watching
2 sit
3 doing
4 to go
5 seeing / meeting
6 have passed
7 losing
8 to bring
4 1 go
2 to do
3 to meet
4 to buy
5 to get
6 listening
7 listening
8 have
5 1 looking forward to going
2 *correct*
3 Should I tell
4 enjoy looking
5 could have bought
6 wanted to go
7 *correct*
8 couldn't speak

Unit 22
1 1 a
2 b
2 was really shocked
3 2 wonderful

3 interested
4 salty
5 disgusting
6 cloudy
7 surprised
8 careless

Unit 23

1 1 b
   2 b
2 was fantastic
3 2 very / really cold
   3 very / really good time
   4 very much
   5 really enormous
   6 very funny
   7 very / really important
   8 really hilarious

Unit 24

1 1 a
   2 a
2 particularly pleased
3 2 finally
   3 truly
   4 sincerely
   5 easily
   6 definitely
   7 fast
   8 luckily

Test 8

1 Adjectives: lovely, shocked,
embarrassed, funny
Adverbs: truly, hard, fast, clearly
2 1 do very well
   2 was completely impossible
   3 I'm very interested
   4 was very bad
   5 is great fun
   6 is really bad
   7 out very much
   8 Carrey's really funny
3 1 selfish
   2 Luckily
   3 musical
   4 carefully
   5 quickly

6 interested
7 windy
8 lovely
4 1 very disappointed with
   2 very snowy at
   3 were bored by
   4 watch very much
   5 is wonderful
   6 is very mountainous
   7 a beautiful flute player
   6 very fast
5 1 pleased with
   2 *correct*
   3 hardly work at all
   4 will be fun
   5 are wonderful
   6 *correct*
   7 quite easily
   8 truly lovely

Unit 25

1 1 b
   2 b
2 an alarm clock which wakes
3 2 *not necessary*
   3 the sentences which are correct
   4 a cousin who lives
   5 the chair which is broken
   6 *not necessary*
   7 anyone who works
   8 A machine which washes dishes

Unit 26

1 1 a
   2 b
2 which is really
3 2 I stayed in the Marriot hotel, which
    was very nice.
   3 I didn't understand what the teacher
    said.
   4 I work with three people who are
    my age.
   5 Tübingen, which is a really good
    team, will probably win the match.
   6 You can come with me, which
    would be great.
   7 I have everything that I need.

8 My teacher, who is very nice, reminds me of my cousin.

Unit 27

1 1 a
   2 a
2 arrived at the station
3 2 b
   3 *both*
   4 a
   5 b
   6 b
   7 a
   8 *both*

Test 9

1 1 at
   2 *not necessary*
   3 to
   4 in
   5 *not necessary*
   6 on
   7 at
   8 in
2 1 This CD, which you can borrow if you like, is really great!
   2 *not necessary*
   3 *not necessary*
   4 Miranda, who's an art teacher, is a great painter.
   5 *not necessary*
   6 Can you see Dr Jones, who I was talking to?
   7 *not necessary*
   8 Our train arrived on time, which was amazing!
3 1 Swimming, which is good fun, is good exercise too.
   2 Agatha Christie, who was British, was born in 1890.
   3 The boy (who is) wearing glasses can't see very well.
   4 Jane sent me an email which was full of news.
   5 The teacher who taught us explained the grammar rules clearly.

6 My mum, who has got a mobile, phones me every day.
7 My friend sent me a postcard, which was nice of her.
8 Look at these pens which I bought.
4 1 who
   2 which
   3 which
   4 that
   5 on
   6 who
   7 at
   8 what
5 1 who's nearly 80, is learning
   2 a pen which doesn't write
   3 you get there
   4 someone who comes
   5 that I'd already seen
   6 *correct*
   7 arrived in Japan
   8 carefully, which was unusual

Unit 28

1 1 b
   2 b
2 'd love to go back
3 2 come
   3 live
   4 stay
   5 take
   6 stay
   7 go
   8 bring

Unit 29

1 1 a
   2 a
2 to go shopping for clothes
3 2 goes running
   3 been swimming
   4 went diving
   5 doing the shopping
   6 been shopping
   7 do the cooking
   8 go skiing

Unit 30

1 1 a

   2 a

2 like listening to my cassettes

3 2 write to you (write you *is correct in*
      American English)

   3 *not necessary*

   4 invited me to dinner

   5 send text messages to my friends

   6 *not necessary*

   7 *not necessary*

   8 said goodbye to us

Test 10

1 1 take

   2 live

   3 come

   4 stay

   5 go

   6 talk

   7 stayed

   8 told

2 1 does the shopping

   2 does the cooking

   3 go swimming

   4 go kayaking

   5 go sailing

   6 been diving

   7 go shopping

   8 doing the ironing

3 1 a

   2 *both*

   3 b

   4 b

   5 b

   6 a

   7 *both*

   8 b

4 1 speak / write

   2 tell

   3 ask / tell

   4 send

   5 say / write

   6 send / write

   7 say / send

   8 ask

5 1 go shopping

   2 write to you (write you *is correct in*
      American English)

   3 *correct*

   4 me to her house

   5 to live abroad

   6 to go there / come here

   7 telephone me

   8 goes jogging

Acknowledgements

The author would like to thank Helen Forrest for her many clear-sighted suggestions and thorough editing work.

Illustrated by Julian Mosedale

The Cambridge Learner Corpus
This book is based on information from the Cambridge Learner Corpus, a collection of over 60,000 exam papers from Cambridge ESOL. It shows real mistakes students make, and highlights which parts of English cause particular problems for learners.

The Cambridge Learner Corpus has been developed jointly with the University of Cambridge ESOL Examinations and forms part of the Cambridge International Corpus.

To find out more, visit
www.cambridge.org/elt/corpus

Designed and produced by Kamae Design, Oxford